# 250 Fascinating Facts about Latter-day Saints

## Rebekah Pitts

CFI · An imprint of Cedar Fort, Inc. · Springville, Utah

Every person or group of people mentioned in this book belong(s) to
The Church of Jesus Christ of Latter-day Saints with the following
exceptions: Cyrus E. Dallin, Elvis Presley, President Benson's chauffeur,
the American media, the Baptist Church, Guerrillas, the ancient Egyptians,
the Native Americans, and 80% of the Pony Express Riders.

This is not an official publication of The Church of Jesus Christ of
Latter-day Saints. The opinions and views expressed herein belong
solely to the author and do not necessarily represent the opinions or
views of Cedar Fort, Inc. Permission for the use of sources, graphics,
and photos is also solely the responsibility of the author.

ISBN 13: 978-1-4621-2314-8

Published by CFI, an imprint of Cedar Fort, Inc.
2373 W. 700 S., Springville, UT 84663
Distributed by Cedar Fort, Inc. www.cedarfort.com

LIBRARY OF CONGRESS CATALOGING-IN-PUBLICATION DATA

Names: Pitts, Rebekah, 1977- author.
Title: 250 fascinating facts about Latter-day Saints / Rebekah Pitts.
Other titles: Two hundred fifty fascinating facts about Latter-day Saints
Description: Springville, Utah : CFI, an imprint of Cedar Fort, Inc., [2019]
Identifiers: LCCN 2018048280 (print) | LCCN 2018053365 (ebook) | ISBN
    9781462129553 (epub, pdf, mobi) | ISBN 9781462123148 | ISBN
    9781462123148 (perfect bound : alk. paper)
Subjects: LCSH: Mormons--Miscellanea. | Mormon Church--History--Miscellanea.
    | Church of Jesus Christ of Latter-day Saints--History--Miscellanea. |
    LCGFT: Trivia and miscellanea.
Classification: LCC BX8638 (ebook) | LCC BX8638 .P58 2019 (print) | DDC
    289.3--dc23
LC record available at https://lccn.loc.gov/2018048280

Cover and interior layout design by Wesley Wheeler
Cover design © 2019 Cedar Fort, Inc.
Edited by Nicole Terry

Printed in the United States of America

10 9 8 7 6 5 4 3 2 1

Printed on Acid-free paper

Every Sunday, over **30,000** Latter-day Saint congregations meet for **worship** for more than **60,000** hours total— almost **7 YEARS'** worth of time.

IN THE ISLAND NATION OF **TONGA,** **6** OUT OF **10** PEOPLE ARE Latter-day Saints— the **HIGHEST** percentage of any country in the **WORLD.**

**HEBER J. GRANT** was baptized 6 months **BEFORE** he turned 8 years old— in a **WAGON BOX** *filled with water.*

**8 BUILDINGS** on the campus of **BRIGHAM YOUNG UNIVERSITY** are named after **Latter-day Saint** prophets, but only two prophets attended **BYU**— **Ezra Taft Benson** and **Thomas S. Monson.**

While attending **BYU**, **EZRA TAFT BENSON** was named the **MOST POPULAR MAN ON CAMPUS.**

THE FIRST **6** LATTER-DAY SAINT **prophets** SERVED A COMBINED **total** OF **28** MISSIONS.

6 LATTER-DAY SAINT PROPHETS ATTENDED THE UNIVERSITY OF UTAH

AND 6 OTHERS HAD NO FORMAL HIGHER EDUCATION AT ALL.

CALLED TO SERVE BY BRIGHAM YOUNG, ZINA D.H. YOUNG HEADED UP THE **DESERET SILK ASSOCIATION.** SHE WAS REPULSED AND HAD SILKWORM NIGHTMARES, BUT SOON EVERY RELIEF SOCIETY WAS PRODUCING SILK.

DURING WORLD WAR I, THE RELIEF SOCIETY SOLD 200,000 BUSHELS OF WHEAT TO THE AMERICAN GOVERNMENT— ENOUGH TO MAKE 12 MILLION LOAVES OF BREAD.

Why is wheat the Relief Society symbol? For 100 years, Relief Society sisters gathered and stored wheat to feed the hungry all over the world.

In 2018, Ashlee Eskelsen BROKE a WORLD RECORD BY 30 seconds when she FINISHED a HALF marathon in 1:47:29 WHILE PUSHING a TRIPLE STROLLER.

Out of 17 Latter-day prophets, 7 joined The Church of Latter-day Saints as CONVERTS.

When SPENCER W. KIMBALL was 8 years old his father baptized him in a *HOG SCALDING TUB*, but stayed outside of the tub himself. Spencer was rebaptized at age 12- just in case.

To date, Latter-day **PROPHETS** have **lived** an average of **39** years **LONGER** than the **life expectancy** for men born in the same year.

President **RUSSELL M. NELSON** and about **1,600** other Latter-day Saints share a **talent—** they have **PERFECT PITCH**. Only **1** in **10,000** people are born with this gift.

NOT ONLY DID **PRESIDENT NELSON** HELP **invent** THE heart-lung machine, but HE ALSO PERFORMED THE FIRST SUCCESSFUL open-heart SURGERY IN UTAH.
HE LITERALLY TOUCHES HEARTS.

FOR 10 YEARS ON *Thursday* AFTERNOONS, **TEMPLE SQUARE TOURS** WERE CONDUCTED BY **Russell M. Nelson**, A BUSY HEART SURGEON AND **father** OF **10** WHO WOULD ONE DAY BE THE PROPHET.

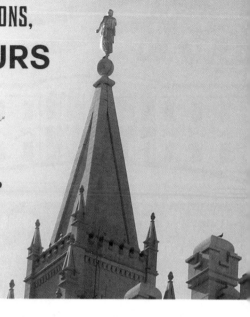

American LATTER-DAY SAINTS perform an average of **35** hours of *service* every month—that's nearly **9 TIMES MORE** service hours than typical Americans.

**SEVEN** *Latter-day Saints have run for* the office of president of the *United States;* *Joseph Smith, George W. Romney, Morris King Udall, Orrin Hatch, Jon Huntsman Jr., Mitt Romney, and Evan McMullin.*

**Mitt Romney** is the **ONLY** Latter-day Saint to **RUN** for the office of **president** of the **United States** and make it onto the **FINAL BALLOT**. He WOn 47% of the popular vote, losing to **Barack Obama.**

Make sure to have a clean face before visiting a Latter-day Saint chapel in **SPAIN—** the Saints there GREET EACH other with 2 KISSES!

It's okay to **CALL** out in **SACRAMENT** meeting in **HAWAII**. Each speaker starts out by saying **"ALOHA!"** and everyone in the congregation responds in kind.

SATURDAY

Saturday is a special day in Israel. It's the day Latter-day Saints observe the Sabbath.

If you visit **Dubai** on a **Friday**, make sure to pack your "SUNDAY BEST."

Latter-day Saints who live there **observe** the **Sabbath** on **Fridays**.

Due to DANGEROUSLY cold weather and LONG DISTANCES, the Saints in the ANCHORAGE ALASKA Bush Branch hold CHURCH over the PHONE.

# SACRAMENT MEETINGS

are held **6 days** of the week in **HONG KONG . . .**

to allow **1,000 FILIPINO** Latter-day Saint domestic **workers**—all with **different days** off—to attend and **worship.**

Need some **GRATITUDE**? Give a prayer in a **SOUTH KOREAN** ward. The members there say **"thank you"** after saying "amen" at the end of prayers during class.

Elders serving as **missionaries** in **TONGA** dress like everyone else—they **wear SANDALS** and **LONG SKIRTS** (**tupenu**) covered with an **apron-like WOVEN MAT** secured with a **STRING BELT**.

To **symbolize** KEEPING **GOD** AT THE **center** OF THEIR **THOUGHTS**, LATTER-DAY SAINT **WOMEN IN INDIA** PLACE THE TRADITIONAL **BINDI**, OR **red dot**, ON THEIR **FOREHEADS**.

IF **EVERY** LATTER-DAY SAINT IN THE **WORLD** STOOD **shoulder to shoulder** IN *Central Park* AND YOU counted THEM ONE BY ONE, YOU WOULD BE **counting** FOR ABOUT

189 DAYS

**MYTH: ALL** members of the Church in the United States are **REPUBLICANS**

*Truth:* **35% of American Latter-day Saints are VERY TIRED of this myth.**

**60%** of Latter-day Saints in the United States receive a **COLLEGE** education, which is **10% HIGHER** than the **AVERAGE** rate of **COLLEGE ENROLLMENT** for Americans.

MORE THAN 3/4 OF

**AMERICAN**

LATTER-DAY

SAINTS

**LIVE** IN THE WESTERN UNITED STATES.

American **WOMEN**, on average, have 1.84 **CHILDREN** but American Latter-day saint women, on average, have 3.4 **CHILDREN.**

One US study found that *Latter-day Saint women* have 1,825 more CHANCES than other women to watch the sun rise—

They live an average of 5 years LONGER.

AMERICAN MEN WHO WANT TO REACH old age SHOULD LET THE MISSIONARIES IN WHEN THEY COME KNOCKING — LATTER-DAY SAINT MEN live AN *AVERAGE* OF 10 YEARS longer THAN MEN NOT OF THEIR FAITH.

IF ALL THE LATTER-DAY SAINTS HELD HANDS, THEY WOULD **CIRCLE** THE **EARTH** NEARLY **2 TIMES**!

# How many massive FOOTBALL STADIUMS would it take to HOLD ALL of the Latter-day Saints?

**250 stadiums** with room for **65,000** people each.

# Thomas S. Monson didn't like Pizza or Cats.

ON AVERAGE, SOMEONE IS **baptized** INTO THE CHURCH OF JESUS CHRIST OF LATTER-DAY SAINTS EVERY 2 MINUTES.

Only **ONE** Latter-day Saint **prophet's** first name was **LONGER** than  syllables: **LORENZO SNOW.**

 of Brigham Young's wives were named **MARY.**

**John Taylor** is the only Latter-day Saint prophet born outside of the United States. He was born... *in* **Milnthorpe, England.**

AT AGE 23, **GORDON B. HINKLEY** LEFT THE UNITED STATES TO SERVE A **mission** iN **ENGLAND.**

HIS GIRLFRIEND, *Marjorie Pay,* WAITED FOR HIM, AND THEY WERE **married** **4 years Later.**

No one will ever know if Joseph Smith would have become president of the United States.
He was martyred 5 months after announcing his candidacy.

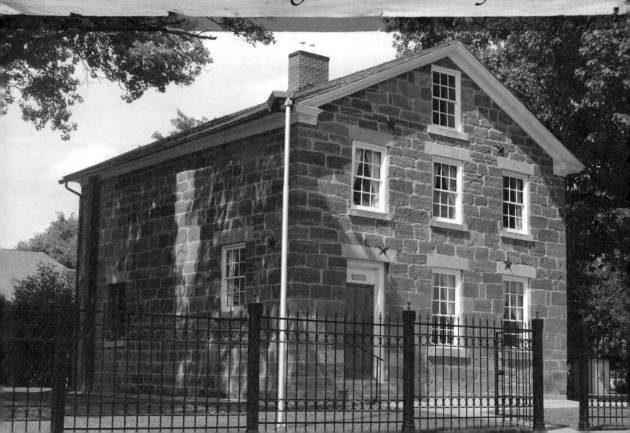

**BENJAMIN PACHEV** is known for winning races while running in CROCS,

But he also *holds the record* as the YOUNGEST graduate of **BRIGHAM YOUNG UNIVERSITY.** He graduated at age **17.**

**MYTH:** Latter-day Saints have **HORNS.**

**TRUTH:** WHEN THREATENED BY THE KKK, APOSTLE **J. Golden Kimball** WARNED THEM THAT ALL LATTER-DAY SAINTS HAVE HORNS AND WOULD GORE THEM IF ATTACKED, LIKELY STARTING THE HORN MYTH THAT PERSISTS TO THIS DAY.

**Utah** LATTER-DAY SAINTS ARE FAMOUS FOR THEIR **LOVE** OF JELL-O, ESPECIALLY THE GREEN VARIETY. IT'S EVEN THE OFFICIAL STATE **SNACK**.

**MORE** PEOPLE BELONG TO THE **LATTER-DAY SAINT** *RELIEF SOCIETY* (THE WORLD'S LARGEST WOMEN'S ORGANIZATION) THAN LIVE IN 57 OF THE WORLD'S 233 COUNTRIES **COMBINED**.

FOR 3 WEEKS, 19-YEAR-OLD **Benjamin Hampton,** A PIONEER FORT GUARD, HAD ONLY **rawhide** —untreated animal leather— TO EAT.

DURING **WWII**, **FRENCH** LATTER-DAY SAINTS USED

Potato Peelings

FOR THE SACRAMENT instead **OF** **BREAD**, WHICH WAS NOT AVAILABLE.

DUE TO FOOD **ALLERGIES**, SOME LATTER-DAY SAINTS EAT **ALMONDS**, Chex, crackers, vegetables, FRUIT, OR EVEN meat IN PLACE OF THE BREAD FOR THE SACRAMENT.

# MYTH: LATTER-DAY SAINTS AREN'T ALLOWED TO DANCE.

## TRUTH: OH YES THEY CAN! THE WINNER OF SEASON 2 OF SO YOU THINK YOU CAN DANCE? WAS LATTER-DAY SAINT BENJI SCHWIMMER.

# MYTH: Latter-day Saint men have multiple WIVES.

## TRUTH: Latter-day Saints stopped practicing polygamy over 115 years ago.

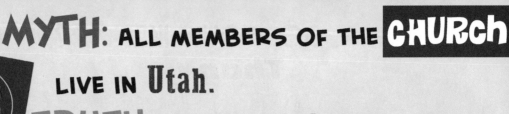

# MYTH: ALL MEMBERS OF THE CHURCH LIVE IN Utah.

## TRUTH: MORE THAN half OF THE LATTER-DAY SAINTS IN THE WORLD LIVE OUTSIDE OF THE United States. UTAH WOULD NEED 5 TIMES MORE HOUSES AND APARTMENTS THAN CURRENTLY EXIST IN THE STATE TO FIT ALL OF THE CURRENT LATTER-DAY SAINTS.

## Myth: LATTER-DAY SAINTS can't use CALCULATORS.

## Truth: Latter-day Saints use all forms of technology, from calculators to robot vacuums. This myth spread from the notion that being a Latter-day Saint was the same as being AMISH.

**POLICEMAN LESTER WIRE** invented the world's **FIRST**

**ELECTRIC TRAFFIC LIGHT** in Salt Lake City in 1912.

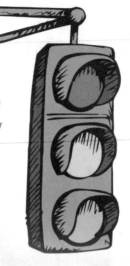

**THOMAS STOCKMAN,** "THE **FaTheR** OF DIGITAL **RECORDING,"**

REAL OLD

12-SABC-DE-6

OLDIES

developed a method to **DIGITIZE OLD RECORDS.**

HARVEY FLETCHER, "THE FATHER OF STERIOPHONIC SOUND," INVENTED THE FIRST HEARING AID TO USE VACCUM TUBES- MAKING SURROUND SOUND POSSIBLE FOR THE HARD OF HEARING.

IF THIS BOOK CONTAINED ONE FACT FOR EVERY LATTER-DAY SAINT, IT WOULD WEIGH AS MUCH AS 6,666 HUMAN BRAINS- 20,000 pounds.

THE FIRST MAN - MADE REAL DIAMOND was INVENTED by HOWARD TRACY HALL.

the world's first LASER surgeries FOR ULCERS AND TUMORS WERE PERFORMED BY GASTROINTESTINAL SURGEON DR. JOHN ALDOUS DIXON.

**WAYNE QUINTON** is the man to thank, or **BLAME**, for the invention of the **LIGHTWEIGHT TREADMILL**, which can be found in homes, **GYMS**, and **doctors' offices** all over America.

Following a **TRADITION** started by ancient **EGYPTIANS**, grieving Latter-day Saints created **DEATH MASKS** of Hyrum & Joseph Smith after they were killed.

While orbiting Earth in the **CHALLENGER** space shuttle, astronaut **DON LIND** blessed the **sacrament** and passed it to himself

while trying not to *float* away in his sleeping berth!

**Don** also brought his **scriptures** on his **SPACE** mission. His copy of the Book of Mormon orbited the earth **110** times, traveling **2.5 MILLION MILES.**

Utah Senator JAKE GARN carried the 1st copy of the Book of Mormon into outer space on April 12th, 1985.

NASA'S first SPACESUITS worn on the space shuttle CONTAINED the fabric GORE-TEX, which was invented by ROBERT W. GORE in 1969.

The *Titanic's* DISASTROUS COLLISION WITH AN ICEBERG KILLED 1,630 PEOPLE,

INCLUDING LATTER-DAY SAINT MIDWIFE IRENE CORBETT, WHO LIKELY WENT DOWN WHILE HELPING OTHERS.

INSPIRED TO STUDY SCIENCE AFTER HIS MOTHER'S DEATH, BIOCHEMIST *Paul D. Boyer* WENT ON TO WIN THE NOBEL PRIZE IN CHEMISTRY in 1997.

ALMOST **ONE BILLION** PEOPLE HAVE RIDDEN 1 OF **HUNDREDS** of rides DESIGNED BY *inventor* SAM Checketts—

BUT HE **PREFERS** TO STAY ON THE GROUND TO AVOID **MOTION SICKNESS.**

Inez Knight and Jennie Brimhall were the **FIRST SISTER MISSIONARIES** called to serve after a policy change in 1898 allowed **women** to *serve missions*.

THE **OLDEST** MODERN-DAY PROPHET WAS **GORDON B. HINCKLEY**.

HE *circled* THE **SUN** **97** TIMES.

Released from her calling at age 93,

Emmeline B. Wells was a newspaper editor, a women's rights activist, and the oldest Relief Society president.

For every *100* Latter-day Saint pioneers to **CROSS THE PLAINS** on the way to Utah, 3 or 4 pioneers passed away during the journey.

A MEMBER UNTIL HE WAS 85, **GEORGE TRIPLIT** WILL FOREVER **HOLD THE RECORD** AS THE **OLDEST MEMBER** OF THE TABERNACLE CHOIR. THERE IS NOW AN AGE LIMIT OF 60 YEARS OLD.

AFTER AN early morning revelation, MISSION *"MOTHER"* Lisa Laycock **PREPARED THE MISSIONARIES IN THE** Chile Santiago East Mission **FOR AN EARTHQUAKE IN 2010. WHEN ONE** struck **MERE WEEKS LATER,** ALL **THE MISSIONARIES WERE** SAFE.

In Japan in 2011, Mission President **Reid Tateoka** felt PROMPTED to invite **ALL** of his MISSIONARIES to a meeting that was meant for just a **FEW—** and they were **saved** from an

EARTHQUAKE OF MAGNITUDE 9.0,

A TSUNAMI,

AND NUCLEAR FALLOUT.

In 2017, ALL of the Latter-Day Saint missionaries in Puerto Rico were safe after the worst natural Disaster on record, Hurricane Maria, Because the mission President followed a Prompting to gather them Close to the misson home.

SHELTER
→

Too Late TO CATCH THE WAGON TRAIN, FOURTEEN-YEAR-OLD PIONEER MARY WanLess TOOK HER 4 YOUNG SIBLINGS and BEDRIDDEN FATHER FROM St. Louis TO UtaH COMPLETELY BY HERSELF.

A BRAND NEW Church meetinghouse is COMPLETED almost EVERY day.

The Church of Jesus Christ of Latter-day Saints was established with 6 members in 1830. 117 years passed before membership reached 1 million— an average of 8,500 new members each year.

**TODAY THERE ARE MORE THAN 16 MILLION LATTER-DAY SAINTS, WITH OVER 233,000 CONVERTS EVERY YEAR.**

Modern missionaries might worry about what they'll be served for dinner,

But early missionaries worried about getting dinner at all—they relied on strangers to support them.

**IF LATTER-DAY SAINT MISSIONARIES WERE PAID U.S. MINIMUM WAGE, THEY WOULD COLLECTIVELY EARN A TOTAL OF 1.8 BILLION DOLLARS EACH YEAR.**

Missionaries today are asked to PAY THEIR OWN WAY to serve the Lord, $400 a month. A young man would have to mow about 480 lawns to fund his whole mission.

THE PROVO MTC MISSIONARIES WASH UP TO **3,700** LOADS OF LAUNDRY EACH WEEK.

THAT'S ABOUT **616** LOADS A DAY, MONDAY THROUGH SATURDAY.

TRIVIA BUFF **Ken Jennings** WON THE GAME SHOW **Jeopardy 74 TIMES** IN A ROW- 54 MORE CONSECUTIVE WINS THAN ANYONE ELSE IN THE HISTORY OF THE SHOW.

When guerrillas hijakced an airplane, Chief Luftsansa pilot **Dieter Uchtdorf** took to the air in **pursuit,** helped bring it down safely in Kuwait, and flew the plane back to Frankfurt, Germany.

While Dieter was a young boy in war-torn Germany, his mother followed a prompting to take her children and flee from a public auditorium—

just before it was destroyed.

AN AMERICAN SOLDIER'S GIFT—
*A PIECE OF GUM—*
enchanted young
**HARRIET REICH (UCHTDORF)**

Elder Awesome
The Church of
**JESUS CHRIST**
of Latter-day Saints

and opened her heart to the **MISSIONARIES** and their *MESSAGE* when they knocked on her door years later.

When President **GORDON B. HINCKLEY** called and asked him to *JOIN* the **FIRST PRESIDENCY, HENRY B. EYRING** asked if he had meant to call someone else. The answer was no, so **he accepted** the call.

LIKE HIS FATHER, **DALLIN H. OAKS** CHOSE TO *NEVER STUDY* ON SUNDAY DURING LAW SCHOOL. HE WENT ON TO SERVE ON THE **UTAH SUPREME COURT.**

The 10 longest-lived Latter-day Saint **prophets** LIVED AN AVERAGE OF 6.2 YEARS LONGER THAN THE 10 LONGEST-LIVED Catholic popes.

THE OLDEST LATTER-DAY SAINT PROPHET LIVED 4 YEARS LONGER THAN THE OLDEST CATHOLIC POPE. ( GORDON B. HINCKLEY, 97 COMPARED TO LEO VIII, 93 YEARS )

**PETER HARMAN** cofounded **KFC**, was the **FIRST** to sell chicken in **BUCKETS**, and coined the phrase **"Finger-Lickin Good!"**

Speed racer **ABE JENKINS** not only set dozens of **WORLD RECORDS** in his **"MORMON METEOR"** — some of which have yet to be beat — he also drove more than **1 MILLION MILES** accident-free.

RELIEF SOCIETY SISTERS HAVE **SERVED** cheesy hash-brown casseroles AT FUNERALS FOR OVER 100 YEARS—

THESE "**Funeral Potatoes**" EVEN HAD THEIR *OWN PIN* AT THE 2002 OLYMPICS IN SALT LAKE CITY.

RELIEF SOCIETY SISTERS IN THE LATE 1800S PAID FOR LATTER-DAY SAINT WOMEN TO ATTEND **medical school**— THEY BECAME SOME OF THE FIRST FEMALE DOCTORS IN THE UNITED STATES.

MARTHA HUGHES CANNON

Early Relief Society
SISTERS in Utah
WORKED TIRELESSLY

campaigning for
women's Rights.
UTAH and WYOMING
were the FIRST STATES to ALLOW
WOMEN to VOTE.

The first **LATTER-DAY SAINT** *to win an* **OLYMPIC** gold medal *did it in style.* Utahn **high jumper Alma Richards** *humbly prayed* out loud *before his final jump and then set a* **world record** *in 1912.*

**WITHIN 2 hours** OF **ARRIVING** IN THE Salt Lake Valley, **THE PIONEERS STARTED PLOWING AND PLANTING POTATOES.**

over a span of 50 years— **1840** to **1890** — **550** SHIPS CROSSED the Atlantic Ocean carrying *Latter-day Saint* immigrants to AMERICA. **Not one** vessel was lost at sea.

LATTER-DAY SAINTS ACCEPT VOLUNTARY CHURCH ASSIGNMENTS, TERMED CALLINGS, THROUGHOUT THEIR LIVES. MEMBERS HAVE BEEN CALLED TO TEACH, SING IN THE CHOIR, CAMP, SERVE MISSIONS, BE A MIDWIFE, AND EVEN GO TO WAR.

THE FIRST LATTER-DAY SAINT MISSIONARY WAS SAMUEL SMITH. HIS EFFORTS SEEMED FRUITLESS, BUT A BOOK OF MORMON THAT HE GAVE AWAY, AND TRIED UNSUCCESS- FULLY TO RETRIEVE, LED TO THE CONVERSION OF TWO FUTURE LEADERS—

## HEBER C. KIMBALL AND BRIGHAM YOUNG.

WORLD RENOWNED PRIMARY CHILDREN'S HOSPITAL, IN SALT LAKE CITY, UTAH, STARTED AS A WING FUNDED BY THE Latter-day Saint Primary Association. CHILDREN SAVED AND DONATED PENNIES EVERY YEAR TO HELP WITH COSTS.

LATTER-DAY SAINTS BELIEVE THAT all ANIMALS WILL BE resurrected AND LIVE FOREVER— EVEN MOSQUITOS.

BORN WITH SPINA BIFIDA BUT FULL OF SPUNK, **AARON "WHEELZ" FOTHERINGHAM** **created** the sport of **WHEELCHAIR MOTOCROSS,** WCMX, **and was the** FIRST **person to** SUCCESSFULLY **land** {3 DIFFERENT} wheelchair maneuvers— **THE BACKFLIP,** Frontflip, **and** DOUBLE BACKFLIP.

Latter-day Saints stopped serving the sacrament during conference as membership grew. Today it would take 12 deacons about 6 HOURS to serve the 20,000 members in the Conference Center. GOOD CALL.

The Church of Jesus Christ of Latter-day Saints

OWNS ONE OF THE MOST SECURE STORAGE FACILITIES IN THE WORLD.

THE GRANITE MOUNTAIN RECORDS VAULT,

LITERALLY INSIDE OF A MOUNTAIN, HOUSES AROUND 3.5 BILLION FAMILY HISTORY IMAGES.

The DOORS to the GRANITE MOUNTAIN RECORD VAULT can withstand a NUCLEAR ATTACK.

The heaviest weighs more than 155 men.

Today YOUNG MISSIONARIES volunteer to serve and receive their calls by MAIL or EMAIL, but in the EARLY days of the church, SURPRISE calls were ISSUED OVER the PULPIT during general conference each September.

LATTER-DAY SAINT PROPHETS SERVE FROM THE TIME THEY ARE ORDAINED UNTIL THEY PASS AWAY.

BRIGHAM YOUNG SERVED THE LONGEST— 29 YEARS AND 8 MONTHS.

Prophet or not, Joseph Smith was not allowed in Emma's garden because his constant stream of visitors...

RESTRICTED AREA ACCESS DENIED

trampled her plants!

On June 28, 1830, **JOSEPH SMITH** was **ARRESTED**, found to be **INNOCENT**, and released from jail *SIX TIMES* all in the SAME DAY.

Joseph Smith translated the 531 pages of the Book of Mormon in just 65 days. Most modern books take between 6 months and 10 years to write.

The CHURCH Publishes Scriptures and literature in 188 Languages.

VELKOMMEN  AHLA W SAHLA  HWANGYONG-HAMNIDA
BENVENUTO  WELKOM  VÄLKOMMEN  MIRË SE VJEN
HUĀNYÍNG GUĀNGLÍN  WILLKOMMEN  SELAMAT DATA
ALOHA  **WELCOME**
HOŞ GELDIN  BIENVENIDO  VELKOMIN
YŌKOSO  BENVIDO  YIN DEE DTÔN RÁP
SALAMAT DATANG  DOBRODOŠLI
BEM-VINDO  BARUCH HABA  TERE TULEMAST

Five thousand copies of the Book of Mormon were printed in the first run.

They are each worth around $100,000 today.

THE CHURCH OF JESUS CHRIST OF LATTER-DAY SAINTS HAS PRINTED OVER 150 MILLION COPIES OF THE BOOK OF MORMON. IT WOULD TAKE AT LEAST 4.6 MILLION CUBIC FEET OF STORAGE TO HOLD THEM ALL.

**Myth:** Latter-day Saints are not Christians.

**Truth:** Members of The Church of Jesus Christ of Latter-day Saints believe in Jesus Christ.

In fact, mention of Christian deity is found on every page of the Book of Mormon.

**MYTH:** Brigham Young believed there was a **monster** in **BEAR LAKE** and donated supplies to catch it.

**TRUTH:** Actually, this is not a myth. It is true. There have been thousands of sightings but no proof that this monster exists.

If you live in the Omaha Nebraska stake, you might be called as the ward

**Gingerbread Specialist**

for the annual **Gingerbread Festival** held at the **Mormon Trail Visitor's Center.**

WILFORD WOODRUFF WAS **BAPTIZED** IN A **FREEZING** LAKE FULL OF FLOATING

# ICE CHUNKS

JUST **2** DAYS AFTER MEETING THE MISSIONARIES.

ON 27 DIFFERENT OCCASIONS, WILFORD WOODRUFF WAS SAVED FROM A LIFE-THREATENING SITUATION —

TWICE ON THE WAY TO HIS OWN BAPTISM.

When President Nelson was born, there were fewer than **600,000** Latter~day Saints in the world and none in

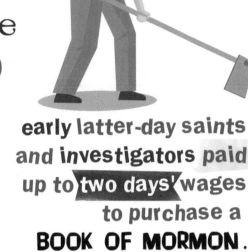

early latter-day saints and investigators paid up to two days' wages to purchase a **BOOK OF MORMON**.

*THAT WOULD BE*

**$250 TODAY.**

SOUTH AMERICA.

By divine direction, **Emma Smith** accompanied *Joseph Smith* when he finally retrieved the **GOLDEN PLATES** from *CUMORAH*,

**BUT SHE WAITED IN THE WAGON.**

**B**RIGHAM YOUNG, A WIDOWER WITH 2 children, WAS **SO POOR** WHEN HE ARRIVED IN KIRTLAND, OHIO, THAT HIS ONLY SHOES WERE **Borrowed Boots**.

**I**F YOU HAD $10
FOR EVERY
**L**ATTER-DAY **S**AINT
IN THE WORLD TODAY,
YOU COULD BUY
ENOUGH COPIES OF THE
**B**OOK **O**F **M**ORMON
TO STACK THEM
**631 MILES HIGH.**

From 1838 to 1976, the state of Missouri had an active

"EXTERMINATION ORDER"

against Latter-day Saints, directing that they be killed or driven out of the state.

12% OF THE MEMBERS OF THE CHURCH OF JESUS CHRIST OF LATTER-DAY SAINTS

ENLISTED AND SERVED IN WORLD WAR II, ABOUT

100,000

PEOPLE.

In the mid 1800s, many Latter-day Saints were called to serve proselytizing missions, but some were also called to serve as

# GOLD-MINING

missionaries—the proceeds were used to build up the

# KINGDOM OF GOD.

Before becoming an Apostle, GEORGE Q. CANNON served as a GOLD-MINING missionary and **HATED** it. He said he would rather do ANY other job besides

# HUNTING FOR GOLD.

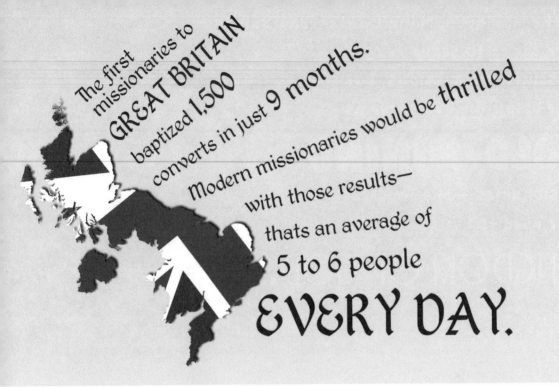

The first missionaries to GREAT BRITAIN baptized 1,500 converts in just 9 months. Modern missionaries would be thrilled with those results— thats an average of 5 to 6 people EVERY DAY.

Deceased since **1960**, **PETER AND CELESTIA PETERSON** still hold the **WORLD RECORD** as the LONGEST MARRIED couple: they were married for **81** years, **10** months, and **16** days.

MOTHER AND DAUGHTER

# TRESA SPAULDING HAMSON

AND

# JENNIFER HAMSON

SHARE IMPRESSIVE basketball careers AND THE RECORD AS THE TALLEST LATTER-DAY SAINT WOMEN— 6 FEET 7 INCHES.

In 1985, VIOLET GIBSON BURNS set a STILL-UNBROKEN WORLD RECORD by TYPING for 264 straight hours— THAT'S 11 DAYS!

Former **NBA** star *SHAWN BRADLEY,* the tallest Latter-day Saint at 7 feet, 6 inches tall, towers 7 inches over **BIG JAKE,** the tallest horse in the world.

WORLD RECORD—HOLDER JOHN HENRY JORGENSEN SPOKE 18 LANGUAGES FLUENTLY IN 2005, INCLUDING FURBISH, MAINLY SPOKEN BY FURBIES.

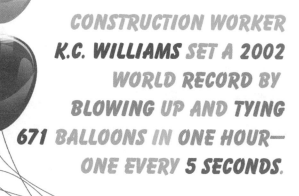

CONSTRUCTION WORKER K.C. WILLIAMS SET A 2002 WORLD RECORD BY BLOWING UP AND TYING 671 BALLOONS IN ONE HOUR— ONE EVERY 5 SECONDS.

The woman with the longest FINGERNAILS in the WORLD, LEE REDMOND, grew them for nearly 40 years before a 2009 CAR CRASH snapped them all off. Her record length of 28 feet, 4.5 inches is unbeaten.

In 1985, at age 10 (when most kids start fifth grade) Anold Sasaki enrolled as BYU Hawaii's youngest college student.

Ace Anderson set the 2003 **WORLD RECORD** for LONGEST CONTINUOUS singing (49.5 HOURS)—followed by NO SINGING for an entire year to heal his vocal cords.

THE TABERNACLE CHOIR AT TEMPLE SQUARE HAS BEEN CONDUCTED BY SNOOPY THE BEAGLE AND DONALD DUCK.

THE WORD "TELESTIAL" WAS UNKNOWN TO MANKIND UNTIL IT APPEARED IN THE LATTER-DAY SAINT DOCTRINE AND COVENANTS IN 1832 AND REMAINS A PURELY LATTER-DAY SAINT WORD.

USUALLY ONLY ADULTS HAVE CHURCH callings, BUT NINE-YEAR-OLD LEY CORREA WAS THE PIANIST FOR HER WARD IN EL CAJON, CALIFORNIA.

In 2001, 58-year-old RICHARD JONES boarded his rowboat "BROTHER OF JARED" and earned his place in history

as the FIRST AMERICAN to row solo across the Atlantic and the oldest man to EVER row an ocean.

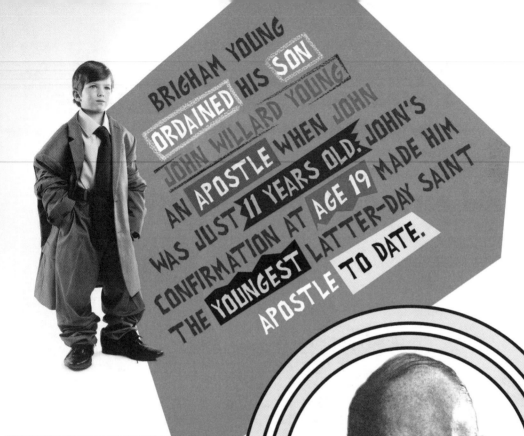

BRIGHAM YOUNG ORDAINED HIS SON JOHN WILLARD YOUNG AN APOSTLE WHEN JOHN WAS JUST 11 YEARS OLD. JOHN'S CONFIRMATION AT AGE 19 MADE HIM THE YOUNGEST LATTER-DAY SAINT APOSTLE TO DATE.

HOWARD W. HUNTER WAS A PROPHET FOR JUST 9 MONTHS BEFORE PASSING AWAY— THE SHORTEST TERM OF ANY PRESIDENT OF THE CHURCH.

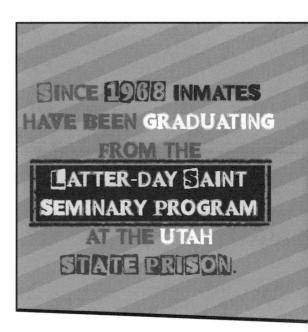

SINCE 1968 INMATES HAVE BEEN GRADUATING FROM THE LATTER-DAY SAINT SEMINARY PROGRAM AT THE UTAH STATE PRISON.

The oldest man ever ORDAINED to be an *Apostle* and member of the QUORUM OF THE TWELVE was GEORGE Q. MORRIS, at 80 years and 2 months old.

AT THE 1982 SCOUT JAMBOREE, 7,200 LATTER-DAY SAINT BOY SCOUTS AND THEIR LEADERS learned THAT whittling AND CHURCH DON'T MIX— 9 BOYS ACCIDENTALLY CUT THEMSELVES DURING SACRAMENT MEETING.

Nothing could stop Mrs. Luett J. Stanliff's BAPTISIM, not even a spine injury.

She was baptized in the Salt Lake Tabernacle baptistry in 1949 while STRAPPED to a STRETCHER.

You're never to old to choose the right. In 1983, **ENCARNACION BANARES RAMPAS** was baptized at age...

# 118.

G. Ronald Carter performed baptisms for the dead in the St. George Utah Temple 5 days a week for **11 years** and was baptized for the **one-millionth** time in 1988.

A CHURCH-WIDE fast in 1985 raised 6.5 million dollars for starving people in **Ethiopia**. A similar fast today would raise over 20 million dollars.

In 1955, President Dwight D. Eisenhower and his wife attended a traditional FAMILY HOME EVENING in Washington, DC— put on by ELDER EZRA TAFT BENSON and his family.

**General conference** WAS POSTPONED DUE TO THE SPANISH FLU IN 1919 AND CANCELLED IN OCTOBER OF 1957 DUE TO ANOTHER

FLU OUTBREAK.

President Ezra Taft Benson holds the record for the two shortest sermons during conference:

"AMEN" AND "MAY THE LORD BLESS YOU AND THE DEVIL MISS YOU!"

PRESIDENT YOUNG ASKED THE SPEAKERS AT THE first general conference (IN 1867) TO KEEP THEIR TALKS SHORT, AND IT LASTED FOR 3 days STRAIGHT.

In the MESA ARIZONA 27th Ward, families passed around ownership of a HAMSTER named Buck but could only "pass the Buck" after giving away a copy of the Book of Mormon or participating in another MISSIONARY activity.

STUDYING **HIGHLY ABSORBENT** SINGLE-CELL amoebas LED *CARLYLE HARMON* TO INVENT DISPOSABLE DIAPERS.

EDWARD W. HOOPE COMPLETED A BACHELOR'S DEGREE FROM THE MERCY COLLEGE OF DETROIT WITH STRAIGHT A'S IN A MERE 11 MONTHS— EARNING ABOUT 11 credits each month.

**Laird Snelgrove**, of **SNELGROVE ICE CREAM**, was the **OLDEST** graduate of **BRIGHAM YOUNG UNIVERSITY**, earning a degree in SPANISH in 2003 at the age of **91**. He passed away 4 days later.

**CLAYTON S. HUBER**, director of **NASA's food** research program, developed a way for "REAL" food to be served to astronauts instead of LIQUID meals SLURPED through straws.

Only one Apostle, **N. Eldon Tanner**, has ever had a **DINOSAUR NAMED** after him— the *Torvosaurus tanneri* or...

**"TANNER'S BULL REPTILE."**

BYU PALEONTOLOGIST *Jim Jensen* DISCOVERED THE **SECOND-LARGEST** DINOSAUR TO DATE— THE **SUPERSAURUS.** IT'S AS LONG AS 3 FIRE TRUCKS— **110 FEET.**

DR. ELBERT O. THOMPSON, "THE FATHER OF MODERN DENTISTRY," invented the Vacudent suction device, becoming the FIRST DENTIST to practice while SITTING DOWN.

MEMBERS OF THE MORMON BATTALION WORKING IN CALIFORNIA DISCOVERED GOLD, STARTING the California GOLD RUSH.

**aaRON ShaMY** set a *WORLD RECORD* for **EXTREME SPEED CLIMBING** at the 1999 **X GAMES** in California. He used his **winnings** to pay for a **MISSION** and later gave up COMPETITIVE CLIMBING in favor of *FAMILY* and teaching SEMINARY.

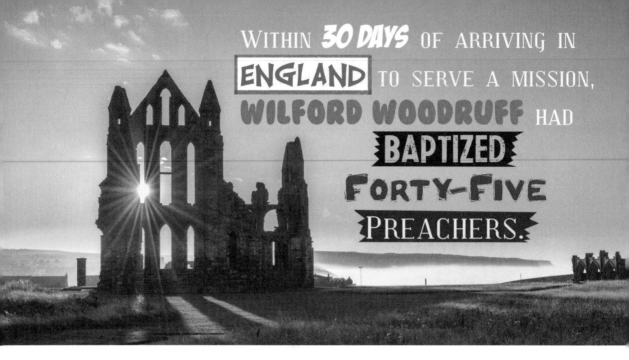

WITHIN **30 DAYS** OF ARRIVING IN **ENGLAND** TO SERVE A MISSION, **WILFORD WOODRUFF** HAD **BAPTIZED** **FORTY-FIVE** **PREACHERS.**

In 1838, Joseph Smith received a revelation calling the ENTIRE Quorum of the Twelve Apostles

on a mission to ENGLAND.

Can you Imagine going on a mission **instead** of starting **HIGH SCHOOL**? Joseph F. Smith served his **first** of 3 missions to the HAWAIIAN ISLANDS

WHEN HE WAS 15.

FROM DECEMBER 1845 TO FEBRUARY 1846, MORE THAN 5,600 LATTER-DAY SAINTS RECEIVED THEIR TEMPLE ORDINANCES IN THE ORIGINAL NAUVOO TEMPLE BEFORE FLEEING PERSECUTIONS FOR THE HOPE OF SAFETY IN THE ROCKY MOUNTAINS.

WHEN BRIGHAM YOUNG SPOKE AT A MEETING AFTER JOSEPH'S DEATH, HE WAS TRANSFORMED. HE LOOKED, SOUNDED, AND MOVED LIKE JOSEPH SMITH.

MORE THAN 120 FIRSTHAND ACCOUNTS EXIST TO BEAR WITNESS OF THIS MIRACLE.

543 MEN STRONG, the Mormon Battalion ALSO BROUGHT ALONG 33 WOMEN AND 51 CHILDREN. EACH LAUNDRESS WAS EXPECTED TO WASH THE dirty clothing FOR 31 people—WITHOUT RUNNING WATER OR ELECTRICITY.

THE 350-MEMBER TABERNACLE CHOIR HAS RELEASED ABOUT 3 TIMES MORE ALBUMS THAN ROCK LEGEND ELVIS PRESLEY:

175 VS. 60.

**EACH MEMBER OF THE TABERNACLE CHOIR IS OFFICIALLY called AND set apart AS A MUSIC MISSIONARY.**

During World War II, **NAVAJO CODE TALKER SIDNEY BEDONI** used the only **UNBREAKABLE code ever created** to safely communicate with the UNITED STATES while stationed in the **SOLOMON ISLANDS**, *PAPUA NEW GUINEA*, and Japan.

Do you love **ICE CREAM**?

At BYU, many students follow a **SWEET** tradition— They purchase **ICE CREAM** for their roomates for **EVERY** first **KISS**.

Myth: BYU students have **NEVER** been allowed to have **FACIAL HAIR.**

**TRUTH:**

**BACK IN 1925, BYU STUDENTS STARTED THE TRADITION OF NO-SHAVE NOVEMBER, EXCEPT IT WAS IN FEBRUARY AND LASTED FOR 3 WEEKS.**

BYU STUDENTS ARE ALLOWED "BEARD CARD" EXCEPTIONS FOR HEALTH REASONS, THEATRICAL PERFORMANCES, AND WHEN THEIR RELIGIONS REQUIRE A BEARD. MUSTACHES ARE ALWAYS ALLOWED.

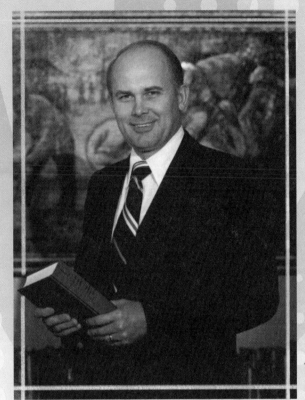

President **DALLIN H. OAKS** was **NAMED** after an **aRtist** his mother admired, **CYRUS E. DALLIN,** the SCULPTOR of the Salt Lake Temple's **ANGEL MORONI.**

**DALLIN H. OAKS** and **RUSSELL M. NELSON** were *SUSTAINED* into the QUORUM OF THE TWELVE APOSTLES on the **SAME DAY.** President Nelson is the **PROPHET** today becasue he was CALLED FIRST.

# MOST PIONEERS TRAVELED TO SALT LAKE CITY BY WAGON, BUT ABOUT 3,000 OF THEM CAME PULLING HANDCARTS.

Of the 10 handcart companies, two of them, the Martin and Willie companies, started late, were delayed and bogged down with early snow, and required a heroic rescue by the Salt Lake Latter-day Saints.

Before they were rescued, the Martin handcart Saints were struggling to survive on a mere **4 ounces** of flour a day— around 400 calories.

The rations for children went down to **2 ounces** of flour per day— about half a cup.

IN 1852, SARAH GOODE MARSHALL carried her **BABY** FOR A 20-MILE WALK across ENGLAND TO hear the message of the RESTORED GOSPEL.

ACCUSED OF STEALING CHURCH PROPERTY,

Apostle **CHARLES W. PENROSE** wrote a **POEM** to help him resist the urge to get REVENGE. It became the song "School Thy Feelings" Hymn no. 336.

CHARLES GOT AN EARLY LITERARY START READING **LONDON** NEWSPAPERS OUT LOUD TO PUB PATRONS WHEN HE WAS **3 YEARS OLD!**

He later married LUCETTA STRATFORD during his 10-YEAR mission in ENGLAND.

*Just married*

MARRYING during a mission was ALLOWED back then. (1800s)

AN **Eagle scout** AND A QUADRIPLEGIC,

## DON CROASMAN NEVER COMPLAINS.

HE SERVES THE WORLD BY **INDEXING**

**FAMILY HISTORY** RECORDS USING

A **webcam** AND A REFLECTIVE DOT

ON HIS **NOSE**.

THE PIONEERS DOCUMENTED TAKING **thousands** OF **ANIMALS** WITH THEM ACROSS THE PLAINS, **INCLUDING** ONE

# SQUIRREL.

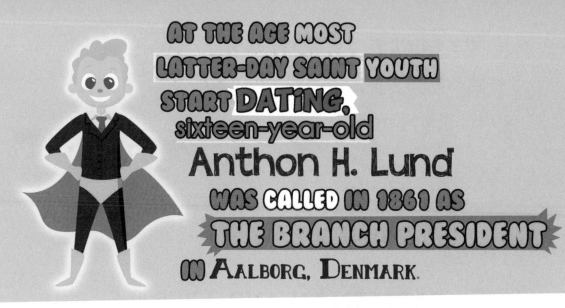

AT THE AGE MOST LATTER-DAY SAINT YOUTH START **DATING**, sixteen-year-old Anthon H. Lund WAS **CALLED** IN 1861 AS THE BRANCH PRESIDENT IN AALBORG, DENMARK.

With a small **MEDICAL BOOK** to guide him, **ANTHON** became the ship's **DOCTOR** while **IMMIGRATING** to America at the age of 18. He was called to the **QUORUM OF THE TWELVE APOSTLES** when he was 44.

IN 1946 VERDELL SORENSEN WAS **BAPTIZED** IN A FISH HATCHERY IN LOA, UTAH, WITH **MOST** OF THE FISH CORRALLED TO THE OTHER SIDE.

CATTLEMAN AND APOSTLE HENRY D. MOYLE SUGGESTED THE CHURCH START A **CATTLE RANCH** IN FLORIDA IN 1950. IT IS NOW THE **LARGEST** BEEF RANCH IN THE WORLD.

Deseret Ranch covers 312,000 acres and is 11 TIMES larger than the WALT DISNEY WORLD RESORT, which covers 27,000 acres.

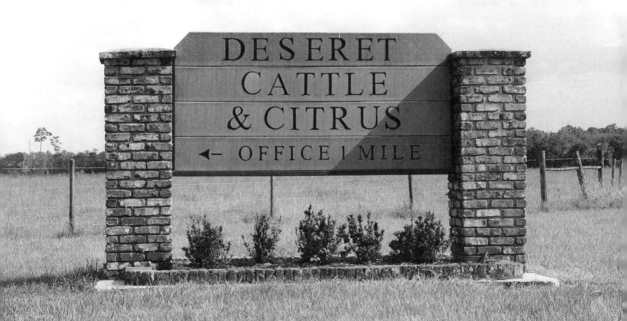

THE AMERICAN TRANSCONTINENTAL RAILROAD, THE FIRST RAILROAD TO STRETCH FROM COAST TO COAST,

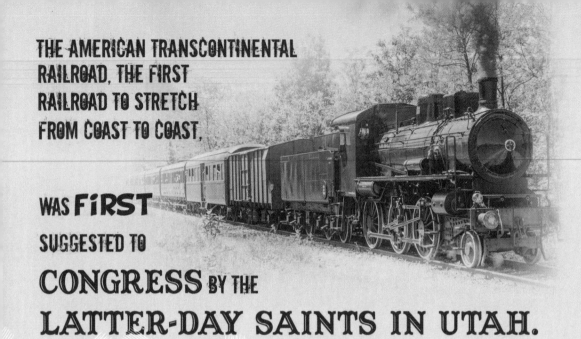

WAS **FIRST** SUGGESTED TO **CONGRESS** BY THE **LATTER-DAY SAINTS IN UTAH.**

TO GET IT **DONE** ON **TIME,** MANY BISHOPS **CALLED** MEN TO **SERVE** "labor" MISSIONS TO **BUILD** THE RAILROAD.

Latter-day Saint PIONEERS completed much of the WORK on the railroad, including joining the EAST and WEST rails with a GOLDEN SPIKE in PROMONTORY POINT, UTAH.

ST. JOSEPH

SACRAMENTO

UNITED STATES POSTAGE

4

**20% OF PONY EXPRESS RIDERS WERE LATTER-DAY SAINTS, MOSTLY TEENAGERS.**

PONY EXPRESS RIDER BILLY FISHER STOPPED TO REST DURING A BLIZZARD AND FELL ASLEEP. A RABBIT LICKING HIS FACE WOKE HIM UP AND SAVED HIM FROM FREEZING TO DEATH.

ALL PONY EXPRESS RIDERS TOOK AN OATH TO TO BE HONEST, TO NEVER QUARREL, AND NOT TO SWEAR OR DRINK ALCOHOL. THEY ALSO HAD TO WEIGH LESS THAN 125 POUNDS!

## NATIVE AMERICANS

SOMETIMES **HELPED** THE HANDCART PIONEERS **PULL** THEIR CARTS... THEY THOUGHT IT WAS A LOT OF **FUN!**

**KIDNAPPED** BY NATIVE AMERICANS IN THE MID – 1800s PIONEER OLIVE OATMAN WAS RESCUED 5 YEARS LATER AND HAD A BRIGHT BLUE CHIN TATTOO. A BOOK WRITTEN ABOUT HER EXPERIENCE EARNED HER ENOUGH MONEY TO PUT OLIVE AND HER BROTHER THROUGH COLLEGE.

EVERY **FAST SUNDAY,** A LATTER-DAY SAINT **CONGREGATION** IN BALTIMORE, MARYLAND, MAKES 500–600 **SANDWICHES** FOR THE **homeless** AND **needy.**

Apostles Jeffrey R. Holland and Quentin L. Cook served as missionary **COMPANIONS** in GREAT BRITAIN  from 1960 to 1962.

ELDER Quentin L. Cook MET HIS WIFE, Mary, IN JR. HIGH WHEN SHE SANG "ON THE SUNNY SIDE OF THE STREET" AT THE SEVENTH-GRADE TALENT ASSEMBLY.

Elder Gerrit W. Gong is the first Latter-day Saint Apostle of Asian desent. He can trace his family history back over 1,000 years to his ancestor First Dragon Gong.

James E. Faust married his wife, Ruth, while on leave during World War II and wrote her a letter EVERY SINGLE DAY until he returned home— more than 800 letters in all.

WIN THE WAR
3¢ 3¢
UNITED STATES POSTAGE

MAIL DELIVERY WAS CRAZY DURING WARTIME. ONE DAY, RUTH FAUST RECEIVED 90 LETTERS FROM HER HUSBAND AND WAS SENT HOME EARLY FROM WORK SO SHE COULD READ THEM ALL.

**THIRTY-ONE YEARS BEFORE** communisim dissolved, FUTURE *PROPHET* AND US SECRETARY OF AGRICULTURE, **ezra taft benson,** ASKED HIS CHAUFFEUR TO TURN AROUND ON THE WAY TO AN AIRPORT IN **Moscow, Russia,** SO HE COULD VISIT A BAPTIST CHURCH. HIS SHORT SERMON BROUGHT THE CONGREGATION AND THE AMERICAN MEDIA TO *tears.*

**NATIVE AMERICANS** helped the first Latter-day Saint settlers of **UTAH** to **survive** by teaching them how to **FIND, HARVEST,** and **PREPARE SEGO LILY BULBS.**

**SEGO LILY BULBS** taste like **turnips**, but don't dig any up for a snack— it's **illegal** to eat **ANY** part of the **Utah state flower**.

WHY DIDN'T JOSEPH SMITH'S FAMILY CLEAR THE **TREES** IN THE **SACRED GROVE** LIKE THE REST OF THEIR LAND? EVERY YEAR THEY *HARVESTED 1,000* POUNDS OF VALUABLE MAPLE SUGAR FROM THE NEARLY 1,000 TREES ON THAT PARCEL.

WHEN GEORGE A. SMITH AND HIS SON WERE SEPARATED BY 40 MILES, GEORGE SENSED HIS SON WAS IN TERRIBLE DANGER AND PRAYED FOR HELP. AN UNSEEN POWER LIFTED 13-YEAR-OLD JOHN HENRY SMITH FROM THE PROVO RIVER, WHERE HE WAS TRAPPED AND DROWNING.

John Henry grew up to become an Apostle and the father of the eighth President of the Church— George Albert Smith.

During the translation of the Book of Mormon, a **STRANGER** appeared to Mary Whitmer and showed her the golden plates. She is the **FIRST** and **ONLY** woman to have viewed them.

While Emma Smith never saw the golden plates, she moved them to clean house and heard the metallic plates rustle through their cloth wrapping.

HOW **MUCH TIME** PASSED BETWEEN THE **first** MISSION CALL TO RUSSIA AND THE ARRIVAL OF THE **first pair** OF MISSIONARIES?

## 147 YEARS.

PIONEER CHILDREN DID MORE THAN JUST WALK AND PLAY. FRANCIS M. LYMAN DROVE AN OX TEAM FOR HIS FATHER'S PIONEER COMPANY WHEN HE WAS JUST 8 YEARS OLD.

● NATURAL FARMING TRADITIONS ●

In pioneer times, Latter-day Saints paid tithing with pigs, chickens, wheat, cotton, eggs, or whatever they produced.

LEGRAND RICHARDS'S **EARLY LIFE** WAS HARD ON HIS **HEAD.** HE SURVIVED BOTH AN **AXE INJURY** AND TWO **WAGON WHEELS** RUNNING OVER HIS **NOGGIN.**

Elder Richards, who was **NOT WEALTHY, REFUSED** any royalty **MONEY** for his best-selling book, **A MARVELOUS WORK AND A WONDER,** which has sold more than **3 MILLION** copies.

DURING THE KOREAN WAR (1950 – 1953), EACH WARD WAS ALLOWED TO SEND JUST ONE MISSIONARY OUT AT A TIME. THE OTHER YOUNG MEN WAITED TO BE DRAFTED.

RELEASED AFTER SPENDING 42 MONTHS AS A PRISONER OF WAR IN JAPAN DURING WWII, PETER HANSEN TURNED AROUND ONE WEEK LATER ...

AND HEADED BACK TO JAPAN TO SERVE AS A FULL-TIME MISSIONARY.

IN-KIND DONATIONS
(THINGS OTHER THAN MONEY)
ARE STILL ACCEPTED AS
TITHING PAYMENTS.
JUST REMEMBER THAT PIGS
DON'T FIT IN TITHING ENVELOPES.

As a member of the BRIGHAM CITY PIGEON CLUB, BOYD K. PACKER helped use HOMING PIGEONS to collect votes during the 1938 elections.

Delbert Leon Stapley TURNED DOWN THE CHANCE TO PLAY MAJOR LEAGUE BASEBALL BECAUSE HE REFUSED TO PLAY ON SUNDAY. He served a MISSION instead and later became an APOSTLE.

Each **PiONEER** traveling west was advised to take **100 POUNDS** of **BACON** per person. That's enough for **533 BLTS!**

When **FOOD** was **SCARCE**, pioneers scraped the **hair** off of **rawhide** and boiled the rawhide into **JELLY**, served **cold** with a sprinkling of sugar.

for 30 years, REED SMOOT served as both a US SENATOR and

LATTER★DAY SAINT APOSTLE.

There has never been another "APOSTLE-Senator."

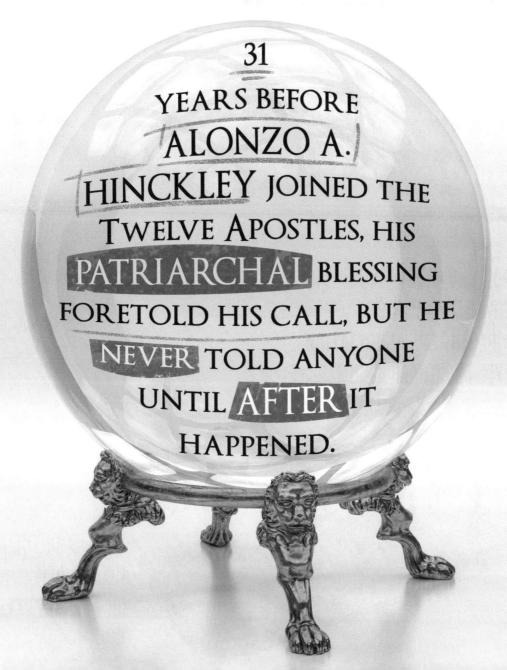

31

YEARS BEFORE ALONZO A. HINCKLEY JOINED THE TWELVE APOSTLES, HIS PATRIARCHAL BLESSING FORETOLD HIS CALL, BUT HE NEVER TOLD ANYONE UNTIL AFTER IT HAPPENED.

Before **SERVING** the Lord full-time, Apostle **Richard G. Scott** designed **NUCLEAR SUBMARINES.**

ACROSS THE GLOBE, LATTER-DAY SAINT MEMBERS OF THE **TEMPLE RIDERS ASSOCIATION** TRAVEL FROM TEMPLE TO TEMPLE

FOUR APOSTLES WERE TRAINED AS PILOTS: DIETER F. UCHTDORF, BOYD K. PACKER, RICHARD G. SCOTT, AND ROBERT D. HALES.

DRESSED IN THEIR SUNDAY BEST ON **MOTORCYCLES.**

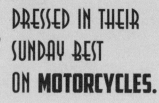

FIVE **SMITHS** SERVED IN THE FIRST PRESIDENCY OR QUORUM OF THE TWELVE APOSTLES AT THE **SAME TIME:** JOSEPH F. SMITH, JOSEPH FIELDING SMITH, HYRUM M. SMITH, GEORGE ALBERT SMITH, AND JOHN HENRY SMITH.

In **SEVEN** short days during the **1850s**, several **Relief Society** sisters started with a **fluffy sheep** and **clipped, cleaned, corded, spun, wove,** and **sewed** a **WOOLEN SUIT** for an outgoing missionary in need.

Six Latter-day Saint **MISSIONARIES** scheduled to **SAIL** home on the **ill-fated** TITANIC missed the ship because one **ELDER** was **LATE**. Choosing to **WAIT** for him **SAVED** all of their **LIVES**.

TITANIC

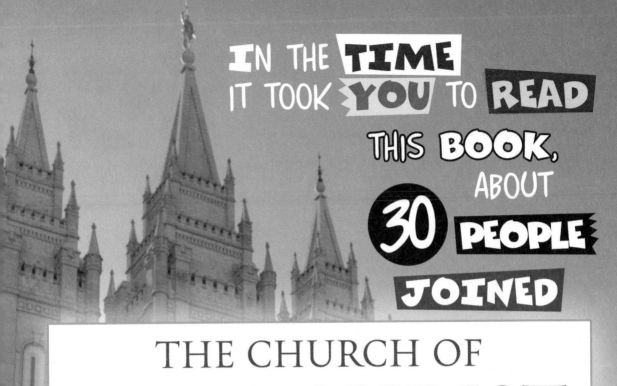

IN THE **TIME** IT TOOK **YOU** TO **READ** THIS **BOOK,** ABOUT **30 PEOPLE** JOINED

# THE CHURCH OF JESUS CHRIST OF LATTER-DAY SAINTS.

I would like to thank my research assistant, Dellory Matthews, for her tireless work, my husband Judson for always supporting my dreams, and my children—Reuben, Tim, Amy, Clara, Audrey, and Emmeline, for leaving me alone for hours each time I told them to clean their rooms. Finally, thank you to Wesley Wheeler for graphics that are truly fascinating!

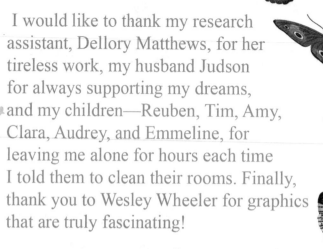

Rebekah Pitts has lived on three continents but in only two countries. She finds her greatest joy from raising her six children on motherly love, large words, and random tidbits of information. Rebekah grew up studying the encyclopedia, dictionary, and, her personal favorite, the Book of Mormon pronunciation guide.